P9-BYR-252

Suddenly Freddy's dog froze. The cubs did the same. They listened. In a few seconds, they heard a faint crunching sound coming toward them. They quickly hid in the bushes and watched someone come out of the woods....

Who was it?
Could it be the drug kingpin?
If it was, what would he do if he saw them?

BIG CHAPTER BOOKS

The Berenstain Bears and the Drug Free Zone

The Berenstain Bears and the New Girl in Town

The Berenstain Bears Gotta Dance

The Berenstain Bears and the Nerdy Nephew

Coming soon

The Berenstain Bears Accept No Substitutes

The Berenstain Bears and the Female Fullback

The Berenstain Bears and the Red-Handed Thief

The Berenstain Bears
and the Wheelchair Commando

The Berenstain Bears
and the
DRUG FREE ZONE

by Stan & Jan Berenstain

A BIG CHAPTER BOOK™

Random House 🏠 New York

Copyright © 1993 by Berenstain Enterprises, Inc. All rights
reserved under International and Pan-American Copyright
Conventions. Published in the United States by Random House,
Inc., New York, and simultaneously in Canada by Random House
of Canada Limited, Toronto.

Library of Congress Cataloging-in-Publication Data
Berenstain, Stan
The Berenstain bears and the drug free zone /
by Stan and Jan Berenstain.
          p. cm. — (A Big chapter book)
SUMMARY: Brother and Sister Bear try to solve the mystery of how
illegal drugs are getting into their school.
ISBN 0-679-83612-8 (pbk.) — ISBN 0-679-93612-2 (lib. bdg.)
[1. Drug abuse—Fiction. 2. Bears—Fiction. 3. Mystery and
detective stories.] I. Berenstain, Jan. II. Title. III. Series:
Berenstain, Stan.   Big chapter book.
PZ7.B4483Bee 1993
[Fic]—dc20   92-31604

Manufactured in the United States of America 10 9 8 7 6 5 4

BIG CHAPTER BOOKS is a trademark of Berenstain Enterprises, Inc.

Contents

Chapter 1
Trouble in Bear Country

If you were to visit Bear Country and wander down the sunny dirt road past the Bear Family's fine big tree house, past Farmer Ben's farm, all the way up the hill past the Bear Country School and down into town, you might very well think that Bear Country was a place where there were no problems.

Well, almost no problems. You might see Ralph Ripoff, in trouble with Police Chief Bruno for cheating people in a crooked card game.

Or you might get stuck in a Beartown traffic jam.

And if you strayed out of town into the spooky gloom of Forbidden Bog, you might even overhear Chief Bruno warning the Bogg Brothers.

But problems like those are not too serious. No one in Bear Country ever lost much sleep over them.

One day, though, a new kind of problem came to Bear Country. It was a much, much bigger problem. It was so big, in fact, that a special town meeting had been called. As the Bear family strolled down the sunny dirt road toward the Bear Country School, they all wondered what the meeting was about.

"It's probably about the Bear Country anti-tick program," said Papa. He began scratching his shoulder. "I'll bet that stuff they spray around is killing the farmers' pumpkins again."

"But the meeting is at the school," said Mama. "It must have something to do with education."

"Yeah," said Brother. "School improvements. New books, new computers, new basketball hoops—stuff like that."

Papa and Mama and Sister agreed.

School improvements were the likely issue. After all, except for Too-Tall Grizzly and his gang of troublemakers, there were no real problems at Bear Country School—just a lot of already good things that might be made even better.

But once the Bears were inside the school auditorium, they began to think that school improvements were not why they were there. On stage with Mr. Honeycomb, the principal, sat not only Police Chief Bruno but also Mayor Horace J. Honeypot himself. The three officials looked very serious. They did not look at all as if they were going to talk about blackboards and basketball hoops.

Soon Mr. Honeycomb rose and walked over to the microphone. He gave it a tap and said, "Is this thing on?" There was a squeal from the loudspeakers. It was worse than claws scraping across a blackboard. "Sorry," he mumbled, and switched to his booming

"auditorium voice."

"Welcome, cubs, parents, and concerned citizens of Bear Country. Mayor Honeypot, Chief Bruno, and I have asked you all here to discuss a very, very serious matter. Without saying more, I'd like to turn the meeting over to Police Chief Bruno."

Chief Bruno rose and marched to the front of the stage. Without a word, he took a small bottle from his pocket, unscrewed the cap, and emptied the contents into his hand. Then he held up something small and red. "Do any of you cubs know what this is?" he asked.

"Candy?" said a little cub.

"A vitamin pill?" guessed another.

"Some kind of medicine?"

With a dramatic sweep of his arm, the chief pointed to the cub who had spoken last. He looked seriously from one side of the audience to the other before speaking again.

"Yes," he said. "It's some kind of BAD medicine. What I'm holding here, friends, are drugs! Illegal drugs!"

A shocked murmur ran through the audience. "Drugs?" "Oh no, not drugs!" "Right here in Bear Country?"

"Yes, drugs," Chief Bruno repeated. "Illegal drugs—right here in Bear Country. More to the point: right here in Bear Country School!"

This set off another wave of murmurs through the audience. When it had quieted down, the chief continued: "On Friday, Mel the janitor noticed that a padlock had mysteriously appeared on an empty locker. Of-

ficer Marguerite removed the lock. Inside the locker she found a supply of these 'happy pills.' That's what they call them. Now, I hardly have to remind you good folks that these things are POISON. I want you all to know that Officer Marguerite and I are doing everything we can to find these drug pushers. But that's just the police-work side of it. Mayor Honeypot would like to talk now about what else is being done to fight this problem."

"Thank you, Chief Bruno," said the mayor. Everyone was listening carefully to hear what he had to say. This was partly because drugs were such an important subject. But it was mostly because the mayor often got the beginnings of his words mixed up, which made him hard to understand.

"Yesterday I called an emergency meeting of the Cown Touncil—I mean, Town Council," the mayor said. "We passed a new law that will help stop this crug dancer—I mean, drug cancer—from spreading to our cubs. The area around the school here has been officially declared a Drug Zee Frone—I mean, Drug Free Zone. Now, what exactly does that mean?"

The mayor looked down at his notes. "Oh yes. That means that anyone who is caught selling, buying, or using illegal drugs in or around the school will be punished TWICE as harshly as usual. In fact, at this very minute signs are being put up around the zone. In addition, Brief Chuno—Chief Bruno, that is—and Officer Marguerite will spend extra time keeping an eye on the area. I trust all of you will support this moo neasure—I mean, new measure—and also remember who thought of it at election time."

The whole audience applauded loudly. Then one bear after another rose to voice his support for the new Drug Free Zone. Mayor Honeypot was very pleased with himself.

Chapter 2
A Mysterious Stranger

It was almost dark outside when the Bear family, joined by Grizzly Gramps and Gran, began their long walk home from the meeting. Papa had not taken the car, because he loved long walks with his family in the crisp autumn twilight. But he was too upset to enjoy this walk.

He muttered and sputtered and got angrier by the minute. "Can you believe it . . . drugs, right here in Bear Country . . . it's shameful . . . disgraceful . . ." he said.

The whole Bear family was too stunned by the news to talk of anything else. Soon they passed one of the new DRUG FREE

ZONE signs. Papa wagged a finger at it.

"Well, at least we have our Drug Free Zone," he said firmly. "That'll make those rotten drug pushers think twice!"

Mama shook her head. "I wish I could believe that, dear," she sighed. "Seems to me the pushers will just stay out of the zone, and the cubs who really want to buy drugs will go find them."

"What do you mean?" Papa bellowed. "We've got to do something, don't we? You heard Chief Bruno. These drugs are POISON! Only crazies and dummies use drugs! Why, if any cub of mine ever . . ."

Sister spoke up for the first time since the meeting had started. "If anybody ever tried to push that stuff on me, I'd slug them."

"That's my girl!" said Papa.

But Brother was old enough to know how hard it could be when some of the other cubs put on the pressure to try something new. "It's not that simple," he said.

"Not that simple?" roared Papa. "It IS that simple!"

But Brother continued. "If only 'crazies' and 'dummies' use drugs, why is everybody so worried that drugs will spread to all the Bear Country cubs? We're not all crazies and dummies!"

Papa had trouble answering that one. Brother's comment sort of took the air right out of him. "Well . . . I . . . well . . . ," he stammered. "What do you think, Gramps?"

Gramps, who was walking arm in arm with Gran behind the others, gave a sly smile. "Well," he said, "I was just thinking about a young one I once knew—not a bad cub at all, really—who got caught smoking johnny-smokers out behind the barn."

"Oh, shush," Gran whispered.

But Sister's ears had already perked up. "What are johnny-smokers, Gramps?" she asked.

Gramps opened his mouth to continue, but Papa spoke first. Papa loved talking about his childhood. "Well, you know those trees with the great big leaves—catalpa trees, they're called—well, in the spring they grow these long, skinny seed pods. You let them dry out, light them, and smoke them, and . . . well . . . hmmm. All the kids were doing it, so. . . . Um, maybe it's not so simple after all."

The Bears stopped on the corner where Gramps and Gran had to turn to get home. It happened to be the corner where Miz McGrizz lived, in her old oak tree house. As the Bears were saying good night to Gran and Gramps, Gran pointed out the ROOM FOR RENT sign that had been on Miz McGrizz's front lawn for almost a month.

"Miz McGrizz doesn't seem to have found a roomer yet," said Gran.

"Goodness," said Mama. "It's been a long time. Hope she finds one soon."

As the Bears headed home, they had no idea that someone was watching them from the deep shadows of the fir trees across the

ROOM FOR RENT

street. Once the Bears had disappeared from sight, the hidden watcher slipped out from behind one of the trees and hurried over to the McGrizz house. Even though it was only autumn and not very cold outside yet, this stranger had the collar of his trench coat turned up and his hat pulled down over his eyes. Moving silently, he yanked the ROOM FOR RENT sign from the lawn and carried it to Miz McGrizz's front door. Then he rang the bell.

"Land sakes!" exclaimed Miz McGrizz when she heard the bell. "Now who could that be?" Miz McGrizz wasn't expecting any visitors. And in a whole month's time no one had come by asking about the room.

But Miz McGrizz went to the door and opened it. Then she let out a gasp. There on the porch was someone with a scary face. He had a crooked grin and an ugly scar on one cheek. Fierce eyes glared out from under his hat.

Miz McGrizz was speechless for a moment.

"What can I do for you?" she finally managed.

"I see you have a room for rent," said the stranger. He was holding up the sign.

"W-w-why, yes," Miz McGrizz stuttered. "I g-g-guess I do."

Chapter 3
Prime-Time Suspect

The next morning was clear and breezy. Fallen leaves crunched under Brother's and Sister's feet as the cubs walked to school. Both had the drug problem very much on their minds. Sister kept shaking her head and saying, "Simply awful about these drugs!" or "Right here in Bear Country!" She sounded just like Papa Bear. Brother walked along silently.

Soon they passed Miz McGrizz's house.

"Hey, look," said Sister. "The ROOM FOR RENT sign is gone."

Just then the front door opened and out stepped the scary, mean-looking character. Brother and Sister gasped when they saw the crooked grin and the scar on his face. They had never seen anyone quite like him before in Bear Country.

"Looks like Miz McGrizz finally got a roomer," Brother said as he and Sister walked on.

Sister shivered. "An ugly roomer! Looks to me as if he might be a drug guy."

"Not so fast, Sis," said Brother. "You can't

always tell a book by its cover."

"Maybe not," Sister answered, "but I say you CAN tell a CROOK by his cover, and he looks like a crook to me. And that just about covers it!"

"Hmmm," said Brother. "You may be right. We'll see."

Sister quickly looked back down the road at the stranger. "Well, at least he's a prime-time suspect."

"You mean prime suspect," said Brother.

"No, I mean prime-time," Sister said firmly. "He looks just like the crooks on television."

"Oh, brother," said Brother. He sighed and gave Sister a look.

With a frown, Sister looked right back at him. "Why is it always 'Oh, brother'? Why not 'Oh, sister'?"

"Oh, never mind," said Brother. "Here we are at Freddy's anyway."

Every day on their way to school, Brother and Sister picked up Cousin Freddy. As usual, Freddy's floppy-eared dog, Snuff, ran up to give them a wet-tongued hello and wouldn't let them go until they had scratched him under the chin and petted him.

Freddy walked out of the house with his instant camera dangling by its strap. Today was camera-club day at school, and Freddy was always well prepared.

"You know what?" Sister asked Freddy. "We just saw Miz McGrizz's new roomer—an ugly roomer who sneaks around like a thief . . . or a drug dealer."

"Really?" said Freddy. Brother rolled his eyes. "You think he's the one who put the happy pills in that school locker?" asked Freddy.

"Who else?" said Sister.

Brother raised a hand. "Now just a second," he said. "We don't really know anything about this so-called ugly roomer. Even if he is dealing drugs, I don't think he's ever been inside the school. He would stick out like a sore thumb. He would have to have helpers inside the school—cubs he pays to sell his drugs to other cubs."

"And who do you think that might be?" asked Freddy.

"Now, I'm not saying I know for sure," Brother said. "But who of all cubs gets into the most trouble in Bear Country?"

Sister and Freddy looked at each other for a second.

"Too-Tall and his gang!" Sister blurted out.

Brother put a finger to his lips. "Shhh! Don't let the whole town know, Sis. Not yet anyway. We don't have any evidence yet."

Freddy's eyes lit up. "Evidence? Do you mean we're going to start up the Bear Detectives again?"

"Great!" cried Sister. "It'll be just like old times!"

Brother shook his head. "No, it won't. Finding the missing dinosaur bone and Farmer Ben's pumpkin—that was cub stuff. This is different."

"Different how?" Freddy wanted to know.

"This could be DANGEROUS," Brother whispered.

Chapter 4
A Suspicious Offer

As the cubs walked along Main Street into downtown Bear Country, they saw a small crowd standing in front of Biff Bruin's Pharmacy. Two familiar voices were arguing loudly.

"It's Ralph Ripoff and his crooked card game again," said Freddy. The cubs pushed their way to the front of the crowd.

"But Chief!" begged Ralph Ripoff. "This card game is an old and honorable game of chance. They played it way back in ancient Egypt. . . ."

"Then fold up your table and take it there! You've already been warned once!" said Chief Bruno.

"Gimme a break," Ralph whined to the chief, who stood with his arms folded across his badge. "A guy's gotta make a living, after all."

"Not by cheating your fellow citizens," said Chief Bruno. "Move!"

Ralph straightened his jacket with a yank and angrily packed up his folding table. He was muttering to himself, loudly enough for everyone to hear. "It's getting so a fella can't make an honest dishonest living anymore!"

Chief Bruno waved an arm at the group of curious townsbears. "Okay, folks, break it up," he ordered. "Don't tempt the poor guy." He walked back down Main Street toward the police station.

"Aha!" said Ralph when he saw the cubs turning to go. His frown was quickly replaced by a sweet smile. "If it isn't my favorite cubbies. By the way, how's my favorite Bear Country sucker—I mean, citizen—Papa Bear?"

"He's fine, Ralph," said Brother, "no thanks to some of the tricks you've tried to pull on him."

Ralph pretended to look hurt. "Now, now, my lovelies—strictly business. By the way, speaking of business . . . ," Ralph leaned down to the cubs and lowered his voice, "if you cubs would like to pick up some extra bread, stop by my houseboat sometime. I'll put you onto something, shall we say . . . interesting?"

"Bread?" said Sister. "Why would we want extra bread?"

"Money, Sis, money," whispered Brother into Sister's ear.

"Exactly," said Ralph. He pulled a pair of fingerless white gloves from his jacket pocket and put them on. "Well, ta-ta. And remember my offer."

"Ralph," asked Brother, "how come those gloves don't have any fingers?"

Ralph wiggled his fingers like a concert pianist warming up. "The better to pick your pockets with, my dears," he said, staring at Brother's pockets. Brother pulled away and put his hands over his pocket. Ralph chuckled. "Just joking. Just joking, my little chum," he said. Then he tucked his folding table under his arm and, twirling his cane, made his way down Main Street.

Chapter 5
A Packet of Pills

As they walked along, Freddy turned to Brother and Sister and said, "Hey, do you think Ralph could be one of the drug dealers?"

"Yeah," Sister said eagerly. "He loves to trick everyone. Why wouldn't he love to trick cubs into trying drugs?"

But Brother shook his head. "Nah," he said. "Ralph may love cheating grownups out of their money, but he'd never do anything to hurt cubs. I think he sort of likes us."

"Well, then, smarty," Sister said, "what was all that talk about dropping by his houseboat to pick up some extra rolls?"

"Bread, Sis."

"Whatever. Sounds to me like he wants us to become his helpers."

Frowning, Brother stroked his chin. "Hmm. That WAS a little strange. I can't remember him ever saying anything like that before. I guess we have to count him as another prime suspect." He looked at Sister and grinned. "A prime-time suspect, I mean."

"You can never tell about Ralph," added Freddy. "He's got more angles than a dodecahedron."

"A WHAT?" asked Sister.

"A twelve-sided solid."

Brother rolled his eyes again. He was about to make a joke about Cousin Freddy's love for advanced math when he was stopped by a scream from Sister.

A bike was speeding straight toward them. It was doing lots of crazy wheelies and turns, and just missed hitting the cubs. In-

LOOK OUT!

stead, it crashed into Officer Marguerite's parked car.

"It's Skuzz!" cried Freddy. Skuzz was a member of the Too-Tall gang.

Officer Marguerite came running over, yelling, "Move aside, cubs!"

"Are you okay, Skuzz?" Brother asked.

Even though he was painfully tangled in the bike, Skuzz grinned up at them with glazed eyes and laughed. "Wanna see me do a super triple wheelie?" he said.

Just as Officer Marguerite called for an ambulance, the school nurse arrived. "You're not going to be doing any wheelies for a while, young fellow," she said.

"Hey," said Freddy. "How come he's got a girl's bike?"

Sister stepped forward and took a closer look. "Because it's Queenie McBear's bike and Queenie's a girl!"

"Oh, boy," sighed Brother, shaking his head. "Not only is Skuzz high on drugs. He's also stolen a bike."

"High on drugs?" said Freddy.

"Sure. Look at him. He doesn't even know where he is," Brother said. "And if Skuzz is into drugs, it's a sure bet the rest of Too-Tall's gang is."

The ambulance arrived within minutes, and Skuzz was lifted onto a stretcher and

placed inside. The ambulance pulled away with its siren blaring.

Officer Marguerite asked Brother to take the bike with him to school and return it to Queenie. As Brother was lifting the battered bike, he noticed a small plastic bag of red pills lying on the ground. They looked just like the pills Chief Bruno had shown everyone at the town meeting. Brother picked up the bag and turned to give it to Officer Marguerite, but she was already pulling away in her car.

Brother stared at the bag in his hand. "Hmmm," he thought. "These might come in handy." He slipped the bag into his pants pocket. Then he pushed Queenie's badly damaged bike all the way to school.

Chapter 6
Under the Grandstand

That afternoon at recess, something happened to make the cubs sure that Too-Tall Grizzly was mixed up in Bear Country's drug problem. Brother, Sister, and Freddy were all waiting for their turns in the daily kickball game when Freddy heard some voices from across the playground.

"Look over there," he said, grabbing Brother's arm and pointing. "By the gate to the football field. It's the Too-Tall gang."

"Probably just got here from playing hooky," said Brother. "And there's Too-Tall himself."

Too-Tall Grizzly was a head taller than any of the other cubs. He was known for being the toughest and meanest cub in the school. He and his gang were always up to some kind of mischief. They put graffiti on the school walls. They rang doorbells and ran. Sometimes they knocked over garbage cans at night. Most of the gang would have been happy to just stick with those kinds of pranks. But Too-Tall wouldn't let them stop at that.

Sometimes, when no grownups were watching, the gang would force a cub to hand over his or her lunch money. Any cub that refused could count on getting knocked

down, at least. Bullying cubs and stealing money was Too-Tall's idea of a good time. The rest of the gang went along with Too-Tall because they were afraid of him. They wanted to stay on his good side.

Brother started thinking back to Skuzz. He was sure Skuzz wouldn't take drugs on his own. He never did anything unless Too-Tall was doing it. He probably got his drugs from Too-Tall. Most likely the whole gang was into drugs! But where was Too-Tall getting them from? There had to be someone else, a big-time dealer—maybe even a king-pin!

Just then Brother saw Too-Tall slip through the gate and onto the football field. He left his gang behind. Brother had an idea. He would borrow Freddy's camera and

climb over the fence to the football field to see what Too-Tall was up to. In the meantime, he had a job for Sister and Freddy.

"You two distract the gang so they won't see what I'm doing," he whispered to Freddy and Sister.

"What'll we say to them?" asked Freddy.

"Tell them about Skuzz's accident," said Brother. "That should hold their attention."

It worked beautifully. As soon as Sister and Freddy reached the gang, Brother darted across the crowded playground and climbed over the fence. At first, he didn't see Too-Tall anywhere. But suddenly Brother heard muffled voices coming from under the grandstand. His hunch had been right. Too-Tall had slipped away to secretly meet someone—maybe the drug kingpin.

Brother crept to the edge of the grandstand and peered in. There was Too-Tall, face to face with someone in a trench coat. The Ugly Roomer! Sister had been right all along! They were less than ten feet away from one of the new DRUG FREE ZONE signs. Brother looked closer and saw that they were exchanging something. It looked like a plastic bag.

Brother aimed the camera and snapped a photo. Then he sneaked swiftly away, hoping no one had seen him. He swung quickly back over the fence.

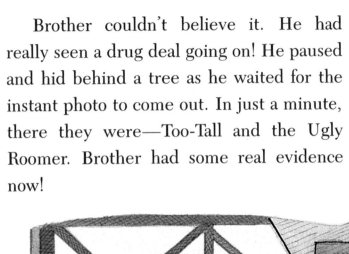

Brother couldn't believe it. He had really seen a drug deal going on! He paused and hid behind a tree as he waited for the instant photo to come out. In just a minute, there they were—Too-Tall and the Ugly Roomer. Brother had some real evidence now!

Brother walked up to the gang. He acted cool and calm. Too-Tall was already back from the football field. The gang was telling him all about Skuzz, and he wanted to hear more.

"Well, Queenie's bike is totaled, you know," repeated Sister. "Skuzz will have to get her a new one."

"No big deal, Miss Smarty Pink Bow," said Too-Tall. "We got the dough."

"Is that like bread?" Sister asked. The gang members all laughed.

"What about happy pills—you got those?" Brother piped up. "I've been wanting to try those things."

The gang members looked at each other nervously. "What're you talking about?" Too-Tall said innocently.

46

"You know—like the ones Skuzz had," Brother answered.

"Hey, what would a mama's bear like you want with something like that? Besides, I don't have any. I'm clean."

"Then prove it," said Brother.

"Ooh!" and "aah!" said the gang members, pretending they were afraid. Brother paid no attention. He was watching Too-Tall.

Too-Tall surprised Brother when he said

"Glad to," and turned his pockets inside out. Some money fell out but no pills. Brother stared at the ground beside Too-Tall, as if hoping the pills would magically appear. Too-Tall grinned as he picked up his money, and the gang laughed. Just then the bell rang. Recess was over.

"Well, tough guy," said Too-Tall. "See you around."

The cubs walked back to the school building. The gang stayed in the play-ground, laughing and joking. It seemed to be a gang rule never to come in from recess on time.

"So, what did you see?" Sister asked eagerly.

"I'll fill you and Freddy in after school," Brother muttered as they entered the building. But the truth was, he was starting to wonder what he had seen. Why hadn't Too-

Tall had any drugs on him? Maybe he had hidden them under the grandstand, or passed them to one of the gang members when Brother wasn't looking. That was still a mystery. But one thing was for sure. Brother had seen the deal with his own two eyes. He even had a snapshot of Too-Tall taking the pills from the Ugly Roomer. That ought to be enough for Chief Bruno.

Chapter 7
The Straight Dope

After school, Brother told Sister and Freddy what he had seen under the grandstand and showed them the picture he had taken with Freddy's instant camera. Sister and Freddy both said that Too-Tall had not handed anything to his gang when he came back from the football field.

"That settles it," said Brother. "Too-Tall hid the drugs somewhere under the grandstand. He's probably already gone back to pick them up. If I'd stayed longer, I would have seen him do it. But I was too worried they would spot me."

"You still did great," said Freddy. He studied the photo once more. "Look—you can even see the plastic bag in Too-Tall's hand."

"And what's that in the Ugly Roomer's hand?" asked Sister.

"Hey, I didn't see that before," said Brother. "It looks like money."

"The money Too-Tall just gave him for drugs!" added Freddy. "It's perfect! We've got the perfect evidence, even without the drugs! Let's take it to Chief Bruno."

"Agreed," said Brother. "But after we visit the hospital."

"What for?"

"To try and get Skuzz to talk. If we can get him to admit he got those pills from Too-Tall, it'll sew up the case," said Brother.

But Skuzz wouldn't admit he had gotten the happy pills from Too-Tall. He wouldn't even admit the pills were his. And when Brother showed him the photo he had taken under the grandstand, all he said was "You

think you're so smart. That don't mean nothing."

"How can he say that?" said Freddy as the cubs left Skuzz's room.

"Oh, he's just trying to make us think we're wrong," said Brother. "Let's go see Chief Bruno."

"Wait a minute," said Freddy. "There's Dr. Grizzly. She'll be able to tell us if the tests showed Skuzz had taken drugs."

Dr. Gert Grizzly led the cubs into her office. "I'm sorry to say he did," she said, shaking her head. "Why, I've known Skuzz since he was a baby cub. Let me tell you, it's a sad day when you see a healthy young cub destroying his health this way. Yes, Skuzz had taken plenty of drugs when he smashed into that car. I've got his blood test results right here." She tapped a piece of paper lying on her big shiny desk.

"Drugs like these?" asked Brother. He took the bag of pills from his pocket and held it up.

Dr. Grizzly frowned. "Brother Bear!" she exclaimed. "What are YOU of all cubs doing with THOSE?"

Brother quickly told her how he had gotten them.

"Oh, I see," said the doctor. "You'd better get those over to Chief Bruno right away."

"That's just where we're going," said Brother. He and Freddy rose to leave. But

Sister wasn't finished with the doctor yet.

"Why are they called 'happy pills'?" she asked. "And there's something else I'm wondering about. What's so bad about something that makes you happy? And what's the difference between happy pills and the drugs you get at Biff Bruin's Pharmacy when you're sick?"

Brother and Freddy moaned and rolled their eyes. "Come on, Sis. Dr. Grizzly hasn't got time for dumb questions," said Brother, pulling Sister's arm. But the truth was that Brother and Freddy weren't sure of the answers themselves.

"Now just a minute, you two," Dr. Grizzly scolded gently. "Those questions aren't at all dumb. They are, in fact, very good questions. Now sit down and listen."

Brother and Freddy looked a little embarrassed as they sat down again.

"First, the drugs that you get at Biff Bruin's Pharmacy can only be bought if a doctor says you need them and writes a prescription," said Dr. Grizzly. "Those drugs are good for you because they help you get better if you are sick. Happy pills or any illegal drugs don't help anyone. In fact, they can MAKE you sick.

"You also asked about their name, Sister," continued the doctor. "It's the drug pushers who call them happy pills to make you want to buy them. It's sort of like a commercial. It's good for business. But happy pills aren't good for you. These little red pills have mind-altering chemicals in them. Do you know what 'altering' means?"

"Alter," said Freddy, who often read the dictionary for fun. "To cause change; to make different."

"Very good," said Dr. Grizzly. "Well,

these pills have chemicals in them that change the way you think and feel. They make you different."

"How do they do that?" asked Sister.

"By working on the brain," answered the doctor.

"Working on the brain? That sounds bad," said Sister.

"Oh, it is. It is very serious. These pills and other drugs like them play some very bad tricks on your mind. They can make you do things you wouldn't do if you hadn't

taken them. Do you think Skuzz would have stolen Queenie's bike if he hadn't been on drugs?"

"Skuzz is dumb," said Cousin Freddy, "but he isn't THAT dumb."

"They can fool you into doing some very dangerous things," said the doctor. "Skuzz is in serious trouble for stealing that bike, and he could have been badly hurt crashing into that car."

"Leave it to Skuzz to crash into a police car!" said Sister, shaking her head.

"But getting into trouble and the risk of getting hurt aren't the worst things about illegal drugs. The worst thing is that many of them are addictive." Dr. Grizzly stopped for a minute and looked at Freddy.

"Addictive," said Freddy. "That which is habit-forming. Likely to cause habitual behavior."

"Yes," said Dr. Grizzly. "The first bad thing that happens after you start taking illegal drugs is that you want more. Before you know it, your mind and your body start feeling as though they need the pills all the time. But the trouble is, the more you take them, the weaker the effect and the more you have to take."

"Is that what they mean when they say someone is 'hooked'?" asked Sister Bear.

"Yes, that's right, Sister. You are hooked when you can't stop taking the drug. What happens is you start feeling awful when you don't take it. And you are losing your health, because happy pills poison your heart and your kidneys."

"You mean they are really POISON?" asked Sister.

"Yes, that's just what they are. You don't realize it when you start taking them, but they are a slow poison—one you don't feel right away. And all the while, you can't concentrate on your homework or mow the lawn or deliver papers or just have fun with other cubs the way you used to."

Sister Bear looked frightened. "Wow, what a mess!" she said. "If that's what happens, why would anyone ever try happy pills in the first place?"

"Well, there are many reasons," said Dr. Grizzly. "But the most common one is peer pressure."

"What's that?" asked Sister.

"Peer pressure is when other cubs try to make you feel silly or stupid for not doing something they are doing. I'll bet you cubs know all about that."

"Sure do," said Brother. "They try to make you feel 'uncool' if you don't do what they're doing. They tell you you're 'chicken' or that you're just scared of what your parents will say. They think they're more grown up just because they're doing something their parents told them not to."

Sister also knew all about peer pressure. "I remember when Queenie McBear first

CLUCK CLUCK CLUCK CLUCK CLUCK

moved here," she said. "She tried to make all the girls feel bad for not wearing her style of clothes, and most of them changed just to suck up to her. But not me!"

"Well," said the doctor, "it works the same way with happy pills. The big difference is that new styles of clothes aren't dangerous, but happy pills are. Lots of cubs who try them know that, too. They have even heard that they are habit-forming. Guess what they tell themselves. 'It'll never happen to ME—I can stop whenever I want to.'"

Dr. Grizzly put her elbows on her desk and leaned toward the cubs. "Remember this, cubs. If anyone ever tells you it's okay to try illegal drugs because you can stop whenever you want to, they are either lying or just plain stupid. Now, you'd better get those pills over to the police station. Scat."

Chapter 8
Tough Audience

The cubs were just heading out of the hospital when they saw Chief Bruno coming
through the front door. He was in such a
hurry that he didn't even see the cubs walking toward him.

"Hey, Chief!" called Freddy.

"Oh, hi, cubs," said the chief quickly.
"What's up?" The cubs could see he wasn't
really interested in what was up, because he
kept walking right on toward the elevator.

The cubs ran after him.

"Wait, Chief!" Brother cried. "We've

solved the drug case. We know who the pushers are!"

"Yeah!" said Sister. "The Ugly Roomer is the kingpin!"

Chief Bruno smiled. "Ugly Roomer? You mean Miz McGrizz's new roomer? Crooked grin, wicked scar, fierce eyes?" He laughed. "You cubs have been watching too much television. Now, if you'll excuse me, I have to question young Skuzz." The chief stepped into the elevator.

"Quick, show the chief the pills and the photo," Freddy whispered to Brother.

But it was too late. The elevator door slammed shut.

"Well, how do you like THAT?" said Sister as the cubs left the hospital. "He wouldn't even listen to us!"

Freddy sighed. "I guess you can't expect the chief to take a bunch of cubs seriously. So, what do we do now?"

Brother thought they should go see Ralph Ripoff about the "extra bread" he had talked about earlier. It could be drug money. Freddy agreed right away, but Sister wasn't sure she liked the idea.

"I don't know," she said nervously. "Ralph lives in that weird houseboat on Old Grizzly River. You have to go through those spooky woods to get there. And if Ralph IS dealing drugs . . . Do you think it's safe?"

"Aw, come on, Sis!" Brother moaned.

"We've almost got the case sewn up. We can't stop now!"

The very thought of more detective work was exciting to Brother. Suddenly he had an idea. "Freddy, let's go home and get Snuff," he said. "I think he might come in handy."

"No need to go home," said Freddy. He put two fingers in his mouth and blew one of his famous ear-splitting whistles. A minute later, Snuff came running toward them.

Chapter 9
Hard Evidence

The cubs went single file along the narrow trail through the shadowy woods to Ralph Ripoff's houseboat. A few of the trees twisted over the path like monsters. The cubs tiptoed past them and tried not to crunch the fallen leaves too loudly.

Suddenly Snuff froze. The cubs did the same. They listened. In a few seconds, they heard a faint crunching sound coming toward them. They quickly hid in the bushes and watched someone come out of the woods and walk past them. He wore a

trench coat with a turned-up collar and a hat pulled down over his eyes.

"The Ugly Roomer!" gasped Sister when he had disappeared. "He must be coming from Ralph's houseboat!"

"That means Ralph has something to do with this drug business for sure," said Freddy. The cubs continued walking.

Ralph Ripoff's houseboat was a mess. It was in a spot where the river became a lifeless muddy pool. The green scum that covered the murky water at the river's edge

coated the boat near the waterline. Splintered planks showed under the peeling paint. Clouds of tiny bugs and mosquitoes swarmed around the houseboat.

"Quick, ring the bell before the bugs know we're here," said Freddy.

Brother yanked on the cord of the ship's bell. The bell clanged loudly. A monstrous screeching came from inside the houseboat: "Pick a card! Try your luck! Pick a card! Try your luck!"

"That must be Ralph's pet parrot," said Sister. "I guess Ralph isn't home."

Brother smiled and said, "To tell the

truth, I was hoping he wouldn't be." Then Brother took Skuzz's pills out of their plastic bag and held them out for Snuff to get a good whiff. "Go find! Go find!" he said to the dog.

Within a second, Snuff was running at full speed. He led the cubs up the gangplank and through the unlocked door of the houseboat. Then he started to sniff everything in sight. The parrot didn't seem to like having strangers in the house. "Off the boat! Off the boat!" he squawked from his perch.

For a few minutes, Snuff was every-

WOW! A DRUG DEALER'S STASH!

where at once. Then suddenly he stopped in front of a cupboard and began leaping up at it. "Good boy, Snuff!" cried Freddy. Brother opened the cupboard. There in front of him were forty or fifty neatly wrapped plastic bags of pills—not just red happy pills but pills of all colors and sizes!

"Wow!" gasped Freddy. "A drug dealer's stash!"

"Your camera, Fred—get a picture of that," Brother ordered.

Quickly, Freddy snapped a picture of the drugs. Just then Snuff began to whimper. The cubs fell silent. From down the trail through the woods came a familiar voice singing a song.

"Oh no, it's Ralph!" cried Brother. "The gangplank's the only way off the boat, and he's almost there! Quick! Follow me!"

"Into the drink! Into the drink!" screeched the parrot.

"Yuck!" said Sister. "It's all green scum!"

"Come on, Sis! Better a little scum than getting caught here by a dangerous drug dealer!" said Brother as he and Snuff climbed out the back window and slipped into the slimy river water.

As Sister and Freddy stared into the yucky water, Ralph Ripoff's heavy footsteps came creaking up the gangplank.

"Into the drink! Into the drink!" screeched the parrot. Freddy decided to follow the parrot's advice. Holding his nose, he dove into the thick water. Mosquitoes rested on his face and his hands.

"There's no way I'm getting in there,"

INTO THE DRINK!
INTO THE DRINK!

RALPH'S PLA

said Sister. "I'd rather—" The front door to the boat creaked. The heavy footsteps started getting even closer. Sister looked out at the murky water and back toward the front of the boat. It was true that there was only one way out. Up over the window sill she finally went, and into the slime.

The four of them swam along the riverbank. Freddy did a sidestroke with one arm so he could hold up the camera with the other. When, at last, they reached a safe spot, they pulled their slime-covered bodies out of the muck. Off they raced into the woods.

Chapter 10
The Only True
Drug Free Zone

Chief Bruno looked up in surprise as the three wet cubs and a bedraggled Snuff hurried into the police station.

"What happened to you?" he said.

"We solved the drug case, Chief!" shouted Sister. "We've got pictures! Show him, Brother!"

Brother and Freddy didn't jump up and down the way Sister did, but they were just

as excited. Being detectives in the fast lane—the super fast lane of drug dealing—was a thrill! And solving the case all by themselves was an even bigger thrill!

Brother showed Chief Bruno the bag of happy pills and the photos. "There you have it, Chief," he said proudly. "An open-and-shut case. The Ugly Roomer is the kingpin. He's been selling drugs to Too-Tall Grizzly and to—"

Just then someone walked into the station. Brother turned to see who it was. "Ralph Ripoff!" he exclaimed. "What are YOU doing here?"

"Hold on, son," said Chief Bruno. "I'll do the questioning around here. Ralph, what are you doing here?"

"THESE are why I'm here, Chief," said Ralph. He dumped a large boxful of plastic bags on the chief's desk.

"Somebody put these drugs in my houseboat! They're trying to make me look like a drug dealer. They're probably doing this so the police will arrest me, figure the case is sewn up, and not look for the real drug dealers. I demand you find out who these sneaky no-goodniks are and arrest them! Now!"

"He's lying!" shouted Sister.

"Yeah!" yelled Freddy.

Ralph's face suddenly looked deeply hurt. "Why, cubs!" he whined. "Are you accusing ME—your old buddy Ralph Ripoff, who dearly loves every little cub in Bear Country—of being a drug dealer?"

"Never mind, Ralph," sighed Chief Bruno. "I know you're telling the truth."

The cubs looked wide-eyed at the chief.

"You do?" gasped Brother. "But our evidence . . ."

Brother was about to go over the evidence once more when in walked Officer Marguerite. She was followed by none other than the bear in the trench coat! The cubs cried out together, "That's him! The kingpin! Arrest him!"

But the chief just smiled.

"Why isn't he in handcuffs?" Sister asked Officer Marguerite.

Officer Marguerite smiled too. "Why should I handcuff another police officer?" she answered. "Cubs, I'd like you to meet Detective O'Brunihan. The chief brought him in from the city to solve the drug case. And solve it he has." She turned to the chief. "I'll go get them."

The cubs were shocked. They all stammered at once. "But we have photographic evidence! The Ugly Roomer selling drugs to Too-Tall, and Ralph's drug stash! And we saw the Ugly Roomer coming from Ralph's houseboat . . . !"

The cubs fell silent when Officer Marguerite returned with three scruffy-looking characters all handcuffed together. It was the Bogg Brothers, the ones who lived in Forbidden Bog! They scowled at Chief Bruno and were quite a sight in their ragged, dirty clothes. Chief Bruno looked each of them in the eye as he spoke.

"Well, well, if it isn't Bear Country's rottenest citizens," he said. "It was bad enough that you were shooting crocodiles and bald eagles. They are endangered, you know."

"Varmints is varmints," one of the brothers muttered, and spat tobacco juice on the
floor.

"And it was bad enough that you were
polluting our river. But now you've gone too
far. With drug dealing, you've tried to pol-
lute the minds and bodies of Bear Country's
most precious possession—our cubs—and
turn THEM into an endangered species.
Book them, Officer Marguerite! And lock
them up!"

Officer Marguerite led the grumbling Bogg Brothers off to be fingerprinted. The cubs looked very confused. "But . . . what about the pictures?" Brother said.

"Fine detective work, those pictures," said Chief Bruno, looking at them again. "Good strong evidence. But the question is, evidence of what?"

"What do you mean?" asked Sister.

"Well now, take this picture of Too-Tall with Detective O'Brunihan. I see a plastic bag in Too-Tall's hand and what looks like money in O'Brunihan's hand. You cubs thought that meant that Too-Tall was buying drugs from O'Brunihan. But he wasn't."

"So Too-Tall isn't involved in the drug dealing after all?" asked Sister. She looked even more confused now.

"Hold, on, Sister," said Chief Bruno. "I didn't say that. Listen carefully now. I said that Too-Tall was not BUYING drugs from the detective. But why couldn't Too-Tall be SELLING drugs to Detective O'Brunihan?"

The cubs looked back and forth at one another. Brother shrugged. "I guess he could be," he said.

"Right you are," said the chief. "That's exactly what happened. That's how the detective caught Too-Tall and his gang."

"Of course!" said Brother. "Why didn't I think of that? That's why Too-Tall had money but no drugs on him when he turned his pockets inside out! How could I have missed that?"

"Easy," said Chief Bruno. "You had already decided that Detective O'Brunihan was the drug kingpin. So your mind forced everything you saw to fit in with that idea. A typical mistake of beginning detectives. Now, let's have a look at the houseboat photo. When you shot the cupboard, you also got the back window in the picture. And we can see out the window to the riverbank. There's something half-hidden in the cattails there. I can't quite make it out, but . . . let me blow up the photo here on the screen."

Chief Bruno turned off the lights and turned on the projector. Freddy's photo filled the screen. The cubs gasped.

There, hiding in the tall cattails, were the three Bogg Brothers. They had wide grins on their faces.

"Just as I thought," said Chief Bruno. "It's our old friends."

Detective O'Brunihan spoke up. Now that he was smiling, his scar didn't look nearly as ugly as before. "You see, cubs, the Bogg Brothers live just down the river from Ralph Ripoff. When you took that photograph, they had just put the drugs in Ralph's houseboat. They wanted us to think Ralph was the kingpin, not them. I know that for sure, because I saw them do it."

"So that's why we saw you coming through the woods," said Freddy.

Detective O'Brunihan nodded.

"Nice work, guys," said Ralph Ripoff. He straightened his jacket. "That gets me off the hook. I'll just be on my way. Mustn't keep the suckers—I mean, customers—waiting."

"Wait, Ralph," said Brother. "One question first. What was that talk about us picking up some extra bread?"

"Extra bread? Oh, that." Ralph laughed. "Just thought you cubs might like to make some spending money. My gangplank needs a little fixing up, and the weeds on my path are getting awfully high. I really don't mind, but my parrot is a terrible fussbudget. All I ever hear lately is 'What a mess! What a mess! Clean it up! Clean it up!' He's starting to drive me crazy. So drop by again. My offer still stands." With a twirl of his cane, Ralph left the station.

Brother smiled and turned to Chief Bruno. "I'm sort of glad Ralph wasn't a part of all this. I'd miss him if he went to jail. By the way, what about Too-Tall and his gang, Chief?"

"We're rounding them up," said Chief Bruno. "Their parents are being called in, and it will be up to the judge to decide how to discipline them."

Brother suddenly felt a little sorry for Too-Tall. He knew Too-Tall's dad, Two-Ton. He remembered the time Two-Ton caught Too-Tall stealing Farmer Ben's watermelons. Too-Tall couldn't sit down for a week.

But Brother didn't feel sorry for Too-Tall for long. What he mainly felt now was embarrassed. After all, he had been the leader of the Bear Detectives and he had botched the whole case. First, he had accused Detective O'Brunihan—a fine upstanding citizen—of being a drug kingpin. Then he had accused Ralph Ripoff of being a drug dealer. Maybe Ralph wasn't exactly a fine upstanding citizen, but he was no drug dealer. This time Ralph had been the victim of a crime. If the police had found those drugs in his houseboat, he would have been in trouble.

Brother looked up at Chief Bruno, then down at the floor. "I'm sorry," he mumbled. "Sorry I messed everything up."

The chief came over and put his arm around Brother's shoulder. "Now don't look so glum, son. You didn't mess everything up—not by a long shot. You found Skuzz's drugs after he fell off the bike. And you got a picture of Too-Tall in the middle of a drug deal. You also found the stash of drugs that was planted at Ralph's place. I'd say the three of you cubs did a heck of a job. After all, you're just beginners."

Chief Bruno paused and cleared his throat. "That brings me to the part you DID mess up, and that was getting involved in this case in the first place. Detective work may be exciting, and it's usually harmless. But this was no 'missing pumpkin' case. Drug addicts are dangerous. They'll do anything to get money for drugs—even steal.

And drug dealing is big-time crime. You cubs are lucky your detective work got only as far as Too-Tall Grizzly and Ralph Ripoff. I'd hate to think what might have happened if you had wound up tangling with these gun-toting Bogg Brothers!"

The cubs turned to look at the jail cell. From behind its bars the Bogg Brothers gave them dirty looks. The cubs shivered.

"I guess we got caught up in the excitement," Brother said. "Once we got started we just couldn't stop." Brother suddenly remembered something Dr. Gert Grizzly had said. "Uh-oh," he said, frowning. "That's a little like being on drugs, isn't it?"

"That's an interesting thought," said Chief Bruno. "I never looked at it that way before."

"And remember what else Dr. Grizzly said," added Freddy. "If this case hadn't been solved by now, we might have skipped our homework tonight to keep working on it."

"Oh, come on!" said Sister. "That's silly! Being on drugs is different!"

The chief held up a hand. "Now calm down. All three of you have a point. A bear can get hooked on all kinds of things, not just illegal drugs. But some of those things, like detective work, can make good things happen. Taking illegal drugs never made anything good happen to anyone."

"What about skipping our homework?" asked Freddy.

"Yes, Freddy, I was getting to that," said the chief. "Cubs shouldn't get hooked on anything that will keep them from cub business—getting a good education. From now on, cubs, you had better leave the serious

detective work to us." The chief tapped his badge. "That's OUR business. Now it's time for you cubs to get home and out of those wet clothes."

The chief asked Officer Marguerite to bring the cubs some blankets and to give them a ride home in her police car. The cubs all tumbled comfortably into the back seat.

Chief Bruno and Detective O'Brunihan came outside to see them off.

"I've phoned your parents to tell them you're on your way," said the chief.

Sister looked up nervously. "What else did you tell Mama and Papa?" she asked.

The chief leaned down and looked in the car window. "That you cubs did a fine job helping us solve this drug case, and that you'll make great detectives when you grow up," he said.

The cubs all beamed. They were starting to feel proud of themselves again.

"So long, Chief," said Brother happily. "I hope your Drug Free Zone program works."

"Me too," said Sister. "But you know what? I've been thinking about what Dr. Grizzly told us about drugs. I think the only Drug Free Zone that means anything is the one in your heart and mind."

"Well, well," said Chief Bruno. He took off his cap and gave his head a scratch. "That's another one I never looked at that way before. But I'll bet you're right, Sister."

Chief Bruno and Detective O'Brunihan waved, and the cubs, wrapped snugly in their blankets, waved back. The police car pulled down Main Street and headed out of town, toward the cubs' tree houses.

As the cubs rode along, their minds turned to one thing. "Detective work sure

gives you a big appetite," said Sister, speaking for all three.

Brother and Freddy nodded. Even Snuff seemed to agree. "Arf, Arf!" he said as he poked his head out the window and took in the good smells of home cooking.

Stan and Jan Berenstain began writing and illustrating books for children in the early 1960s, when their two young sons were beginning to read. That marked the start of the best-selling Berenstain Bears series. Now, with more than 95 books in print, videos, television shows, and even a Berenstain Bears theme park, it's hard to tell where the Bears end and the Berenstains begin!

Stan and Jan make their home in Bucks County, Pennsylvania, and plan on writing and illustrating many more books for children, especially for their four grandchildren, who keep them well in touch with the kids of today.